JOBS IN SCIENCE

PETER TURNER

WORKING IN AUSTRALIA

REDBACK publishing

First published 2022 by
Redback Publishing
Australia

www.redbackpublishing.com.au
orders@redbackpublishing.com.au

ISBN 978-1-761400-36-0 PBK

Author: Peter Turner
Editor: Caroline Thomas
Designer: Redback Publishing

A catalogue record for this book is available from the National Library of Australia

Original illustrations © Redback Publishing 2024
Originated by Redback Publishing

Acknowledgements
Abbreviations: l—left, r—right, b—bottom, t—top, c—centre, m—middle
We would like to thank the following for permission to reproduce photographs: (Images © shutterstock)

p2b, ChameleonsEye / Shutterstock.com ,
p11tr, Alexey Rezvykh / Shutterstock.com,
P21TR, Sebastian stocking / Shutterstock.com,
21B, Edward Haylan / Shutterstock.com,
23tr, Orion Media Group / Shutterstock.com,
p27t, Nicolas Economou / Shutterstock.com,
p29t, KrisDurlen / Shutterstock.com,

CONTENTS

SCIENCE IN AUSTRALIA

When you think of science, the image of a scientist in a white coat might be what first springs to mind. But science doesn't just take place in laboratories. There are a variety of jobs in many areas of science ranging from work in laboratories, to inspecting foods for export, developing computer software, and developing and testing new medicines. In Australia, science is a rapidly growing field.

WORK TYPES

KEY AREAS IN SCIENCE

- Earth, environment and weather sciences
- sports and food sciences
- medical, social and animal sciences
- computer science
- various support and administrative roles

KEY SKILLS FOR SCIENTISTS

- ***strong maths abilities*** – for working with lots of calculations and large amounts of data
- ***curiosity*** – to discover the unknown and question existing knowledge
- ***good IT skills*** – you may need to work with cutting edge technology and advanced equipment
- ***good communication skills*** – you will need to write scientific reports and explain your work to non-scientists

SCIENTIFIC ACHIEVEMENTS

Many ground-breaking scientific discoveries have been made in Australia. The Australian Government, as well as various commercial industries, invest a lot of money in scientific research. Scientists at the Australian Institute of Sport have developed cooling technologies that are now used by athletes around the world, while Australian medical scientists have developed life-saving medicines and vaccines that are making enormous contributions to people across the globe.

RUSH TO PUBLISH

In many scientific fields, particularly medical science, great importance is placed on publishing discoveries in international scientific journals. By publishing their results, scientists are able to share their research with the scientific community and become recognised for their discoveries. This allows other scientists from all over the world to read their published reports, analyse their research and comment or expand on the ideas and discoveries presented.

WORKING OVERSEAS

Many Australian scientists work overseas at some point in their careers and Australian scientists are well regarded in the international scientific community. It can be very useful for scientists to gain experience and skills overseas and to share their skills abroad. Australia is a leader in scientific research in many fields and this attracts overseas scientists. These scientists bring new knowledge, skills and expertise to Australia.

MEDICAL SCIENCE

MEDICAL SCIENTIST

JOB DESCRIPTION

Medical scientists conduct laboratory tests that lead to the diagnosis, treatment, cure and prevention of diseases. This can involve analysing blood, tissue and urine samples, or examining genetic material such as DNA. Medical scientists might also grow disease-causing organisms such as bacteria and viruses to examine and better understand them. Medical scientists publish their results in medical journals and present their findings to doctors, pharmaceutical companies and other health professionals. Scientists working on the development of drugs might be involved in testing the drugs on animals including mice, rats and rabbits.

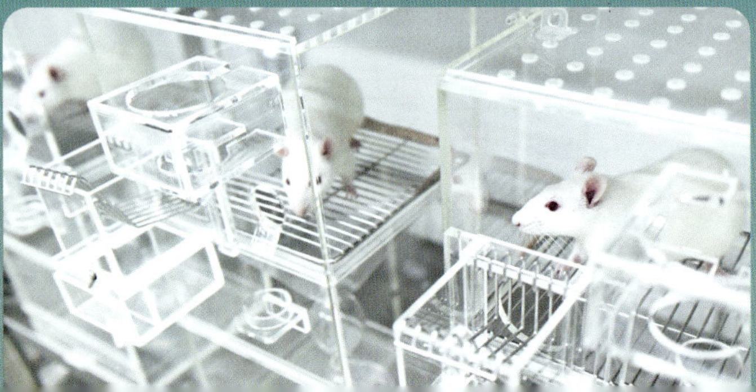

Medical science involves research into the nature and causes of diseases. This research enables scientists to develop cures and preventions including drugs, vaccines and other treatments such as radiotherapy.

RANGE OF SPECIALITIES:

- ***haematology*** – research into diseases of the blood
- ***immunology*** – research into the immune system
- ***microbiology*** – research into infections and how they cause illnesses
- ***cytology*** – research into cancer cells

EDUCATION AND TRAINING

Medical scientists require a science degree. Most medical scientists, especially those who have specialised, have postgraduate qualifications in the area of their specialty.

MEDICAL RESEARCH ASSISTANT

JOB DESCRIPTION

Medical research assistants conduct laboratory tests under the supervision of senior scientists. They are also responsible for recording details of the experiments and ensuring equipment is kept clean.

EDUCATION AND TRAINING

Medical research assistants need a science degree. An additional honours year can be helpful in getting a job, as there is a lot of competition for research assistant positions. Many important working techniques are taught on-the-job.

MY STORY

I work in a laboratory that looks at abnormalities in DNA. My job involves preparing the tissue samples from organs for scientific analysis. This work involves many complex processes and I need to use toxic chemicals and scientific instruments. I also help with the organisation and maintenance of the laboratory and its equipment.

Each day, I make detailed notes on all the experiments we conduct, so that when we discover something important, we have evidence to prove that correct scientific methods were used. I like that I am able to learn so many different techniques and I especially enjoy teaching new techniques to other people. I also like designing my own experiments and seeing them work.

A few words of advice:
The best way to get a head start in biological science is to apply for work experience while you are studying. Quite often this can lead to getting a scholarship, especially if you show you are enthusiastic and eager to learn.

AMY HERLIHY
RESEARCH ASSISTANT

'apply for work experience while you are studying'

PHARMACIST

JOB DESCRIPTION

Pharmacists supply, dispense and manufacture medicines and drugs in hospitals and community pharmacies. They advise patients on the appropriate use of the medicines as well as any side effects they may cause. Some pharmacists also conduct research into the formulation, production, storage, quality control and distribution of medicines and drugs.

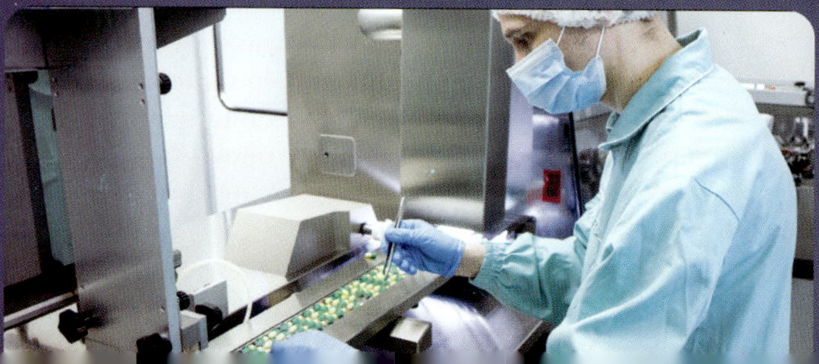

RANGE OF WORK:

- prepare medicines in various forms, such as in capsules or ointments
- advise patients on how to take their medicines
- advise other health professionals and members of the public about medicines
- develop standards that will be legally recognised and regulated
- offer advice on Government controls and regulations concerning the manufacture and supply of medicines

EDUCATION AND TRAINING

To become a pharmacist, you will need to complete a university degree in pharmacy, followed by a one-year internship.

MEDICAL LABORATORY TECHNICIAN

JOB DESCRIPTION

Medical laboratory technicians carry out routine tests and other procedures for diagnosing and treating diseases. Their tasks include setting up equipment and keeping it clean, preparing tissue or blood samples for examination under a microscope, collecting blood samples, and communicating results to medical scientists. Medical laboratory technicians need to pay attention to detail and be able to do repetitive work without losing concentration.

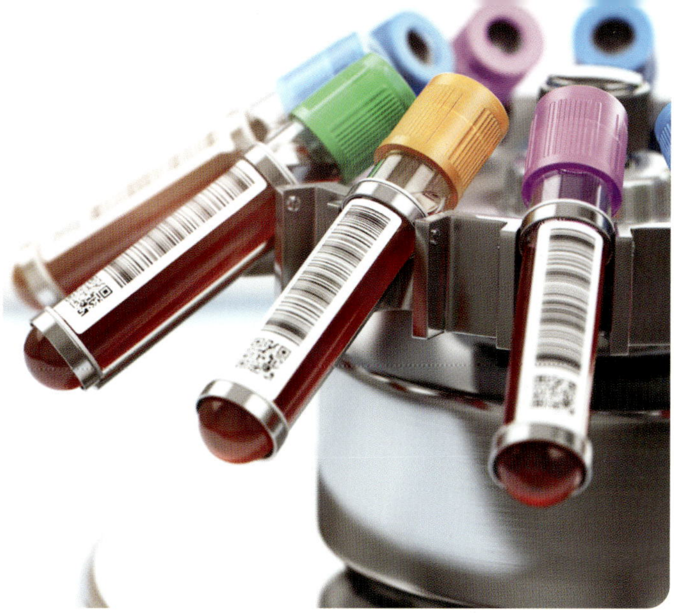

EDUCATION AND TRAINING

It may be possible to become a medical laboratory technician with school qualifications. However, TAFE qualifications in laboratory techniques are usually required.

MY STORY

'I knew … I did not want to be a doctor or a nurse'

I became interested in medical science when I was about 14. My brother was a very sick child and he was always going to hospital. I remember watching the doctors and nurses and being fascinated. I knew, though, that I did not want to be a doctor or nurse. It was the science behind what they were doing that interested me. I started researching my brother's condition and started to talk to the doctors about it. They told me a lot about the new research that was being done. I was hooked.

Being a lab technician allows me to conduct scientific experiments, but not have to be under too much pressure. The medical scientists discuss their experiments with me and we decide on the things I can do without supervision. I am then in charge of those parts of the experiment. Often, I need to repeat the same procedure several times to make sure I always get the same, or a similar, result.

A few words of advice:
Only become a lab technician if you're sure you don't want to be in charge of complete experiments. A lot of the work involves being told what to do by senior scientists so you need to be able to listen and follow instructions.

SUE GIBBS
MEDICAL LABORATORY TECHNICIAN

EARTH SCIENCES

Many of the resources used to make products come from beneath the Earth's surface. Earth sciences are concerned with locating and extracting minerals and other materials from the Earth. Earth scientists work for mining companies, universities and Government departments.

• GEOLOGIST

JOB DESCRIPTION

Geologists study the different types of rocks that make up the Earth's crust. The structure of different rock types can help scientists to locate minerals and provide advice to mining companies on how best to extract them from the ground. Geologists work in laboratories and offices, as well as out in the field. They often work in remote regions.

RANGE OF WORK:

- cut fossils and rock samples
- locate and manage groundwater resources
- examine geological specimens in laboratories
- prepare geological models to make predictions

EDUCATION AND TRAINING

To become a geologist, you need at least a bachelor's degree in geology, Earth science, or a related field. A science degree with a major in geology, an honours year and any further postgraduate study might enhance employment opportunities. Geologists need to be physically fit, interested in technical and engineering work and be prepared to work outdoors in a range of environments.

GEOPHYSICIST

JOB DESCRIPTION

Geophysicists are concerned with what's going on below the ground. They study magnetism, gravity and electrical impulses through field surveys. They also conduct a range of scientific testing that includes seismic testing. Geophysicists need a high level of knowledge of physics and mathematics and they need to be interested in technical and engineering work. Many geophysicists work for mining companies.

EDUCATION AND TRAINING

To become a geophysicist, you need a minimum of a bachelor's degree in geophysics or geosciences. An honours degree or postgraduate qualifications such as a master's degree will greatly improve employment opportunities.

METALLURGIST

JOB DESCRIPTION

Metallurgists study minerals and investigate different ways of processing minerals. They use a variety of methods to separate minerals from their ores, and look for the most efficient way to extract minerals in large quantities.

EDUCATION AND TRAINING

Metallurgists need an engineering degree with a major in metallurgy or materials.

MY STORY

I started off working at an open pit mine in far north Queensland. My role included geological mapping, structural and rock mass analyses, and general mine operations work. My work was to inspect and analyse the rock to make the conditions safe. I reported any problems I found to the mine manager with recommendations on how to manage the situation. After about 12 months, I realised that mining was not for me. There are long hours involved and you spend most of your time interstate, away from home.

I now work in the civil geotechnical area. This involves inspecting, testing and designing any footings that are supported by rock or soil for any type of structure. Footings are the foundations that a structure is built on. I spend most of my time on-site inspecting and testing to ensure that the job is completed to requirements. I use maps, soil and rock data, and special testing devices to determine the properties of the soil and rocks. This data is then used to recommend the type of footings required for the building or structure.

A few words of advice:
Make sure you want to work in and enjoy the outdoors, and that you're prepared and happy to travel.

DION DENES
GEOTECHNICAL ENGINEER

'Make sure you want to work in and enjoy the outdoors'

ENVIRONMENTAL SCIENCE

Environmental science covers a broad range of occupations. The demand for scientific knowledge and skills in areas involving the management and protection of the natural environment is growing. Many environmental scientists work for the Government in policy development roles, and many work out in the field.

• MARINE BIOLOGIST

JOB DESCRIPTION

Marine biologists study all forms of life in the sea, how they interact with one another and how they are affected by environmental changes. Marine biologists work in laboratories, in offices, at sea, or in shore based field stations.

RANGE OF WORK:

- estimate numbers of marine organisms
- carry out environmental studies and create impact reports on any changes to marine life
- monitor pollution
- write scientific reports and make recommendations for marine conservation

EDUCATION AND TRAINING

To become a marine biologist, you have to study science or applied science at university with a major in marine biology or marine science. You may also consider major streams that emphasise marine biology such as aquaculture and environmental biology. Postgraduate qualifications such as a master's degree are generally required to progress in this career path.

• ENVIRONMENTAL SCIENTIST

JOB DESCRIPTION

Environmental scientists work to control or minimise the harmful effects of human activity on the environment. Environmental scientists work both in laboratories and in the field. They use scientific methods to record the ways human activities affect the environment. For example, they might test the water quality of a stream before and after logging. This information helps industry and the Government to develop policies for environmentally sustainable industries and developments. Environmental scientists can specialise in a variety of areas including hydrology, air quality, forestry and waste management.

EDUCATION AND TRAINING

A science degree with a major in geography or environmental science is the main requirement for work in this area. Postgraduate qualifications will be required to specialise.

WATER AND WASTEWATER PLANT OPERATOR

JOB DESCRIPTION

Water and wastewater plant operators control the pumping of water for supply and storage, and treat water to purify it or remove waste.

RANGE OF WORK:

- receive, load and unload chemicals
- take samples for analysis
- operate pumps and valves to control flowing water
- regulate water flows during treatments
- operate water purification equipment

EDUCATION AND TRAINING

To become a water and wastewater plant operator, you usually need to have completed a traineeship or apprenticeship in water industry operations.

BOTANIST

JOB DESCRIPTION

Botanists study the biology of plants. They examine the impact of environmental factors on plant growth, such as rainfall, temperature, sunlight and soil conditions. They might also work with other scientists to develop drugs and other products from plants. They can help to regenerate plant life in an area that has been mined, or advise Governments on environmental issues. Botanists can work in the agricultural field, forestry, horticulture or medicine.

EDUCATION AND TRAINING

To become a botanist, you usually need a bachelor's degree or higher in botany, horticulture, plant sciences, ecology, or environmental science.

MY STORY

The work I do is mainly research into how people affect the natural water cycle - specifically water in rivers. River environments are incredibly complex. I do a lot of field work where I watch the patterns made by water flowing over rocks, around bends and through pools. I take measurements in rivers and then build mathematical models of the river's flow behaviour. I spend a lot of time analysing data on a computer, and then publish the results to contribute to the field of knowledge of river flows. I report my results to Government agencies. These results help in their policy and management decisions regarding rivers.

Another part of my work is to supervise research students. I act as a mentor to them and help them with any problems they might have. I like working with students and other environmental scientists.

A few words of advice:
If you enjoy rivers then take a closer look at the flow patterns within the river channel. Our knowledge of water movement in natural rivers is pretty limited and maybe you could help to extend this knowledge base in the future.

MICHAEL STEWARDSON
HYDROLOGIST

'River environments are incredibly complex.'

SPORTS SCIENCE

The role of science in elite sport is continually growing. Australians are successful in many sports and one of the reasons behind this is the application of science.

• SPORTS SCIENTIST

JOB DESCRIPTION

Sports scientists help sportspeople to achieve their best possible sporting performance. They perform fitness tests on athletes to determine how their bodies work, and to develop ways to maximise their performance. Sports scientists also work to ensure athletes' bodies are moving smoothly in order to prevent injuries. They often work with coaches to improve an athlete's performances.

RANGE OF SPECIALITIES:

- ***medicine*** – treating injuries and illness
- ***physiology*** – improving how the body works
- ***nutrition*** – providing the best foods and supplements for high performance
- ***psychology*** – working on mental preparations
- ***biomechanics*** – analysing and improving body movements

EDUCATION AND TRAINING

Sports scientists need a degree in applied science, human movement science, or exercise/sports science.

• SPORTS DIETITIAN

JOB DESCRIPTION

Sports dietitians apply the science of nutrition to help elite sportspeople perform at their best. They make sure the diets of individual athletes suit their needs for maximum performance in their particular sports. Sports dietitians educate sportspeople in how to prepare the kinds of foods their bodies require, and plan diets for them.

EDUCATION AND TRAINING

To become a dietitian you need a degree in applied science or a degree in nutrition and dietetics. As it is a competitive field, most sports dietitians have postgraduate qualifications. Dietitians with lots of experience working with athletes are considered sports dietitians, although you may also specialise in sports nutrition at postgraduate level.

• SPORTS PSYCHOLOGIST

JOB DESCRIPTION

Sports psychologists work with athletes to ensure they are mentally prepared for elite competition. They usually work with individual athletes though they can work with a team.

RANGE OF WORK:

- advise on ways to improve concentration
- advise on stress management
- advise on ways to achieve positive thinking
- advise on how to perform under pressure

EDUCATION AND TRAINING

Sport psychologists need to complete a degree in psychology. Most positions will require a postgraduate psychology degree with an emphasis on sports psychology.

• BIOMECHANIST

JOB DESCRIPTION

Biomechanics is concerned with forces and how they interact with the human body. Biomechanists analyse athletes' techniques using high-tech equipment to determine strengths and weaknesses in their movement. Together with the coach and athlete, a biomechanist can tailor the athlete's movements to improve performance and technique.

RANGE OF WORK:

- advise on ways to improve concentration
- determine strengths and weaknesses in an athlete's movement
- work with athletes and coaches to perfect athletes' techniques

EDUCATION AND TRAINING

Biomechanists need a degree in human movement, kinesiology, or mechanical engineering, and a postgraduate qualification in biomechanics.

'a background in physics and maths is an advantage'

MY STORY

I analyse an athlete's technique to help make their movements more efficient. This might help a cricketer to bowl faster, a kayaker to paddle faster, a swimmer to swim faster, or a hockey player to hit the ball harder. Many sports at the AIS use biomechanics to assist with improving performance. Efficient movement also generally reduces the chance of injury. Some of my work is with physiotherapists, helping to reduce the chances of injury or identify the cause of an injury. We use high-tech equipment such as high speed video, force plates, and telemetry systems to measure and analyse what an athlete is doing in their training and competitive environment.

A great part of the job is working with very motivated people and seeing athletes and coaches achieve their goals.

A few words of advice:
Having a background in physics and maths is an advantage and university level engineering subjects can also be helpful.

JOHN BAKER
BIOMECHANIST
AUSTRALIA INSTITUTE OF SPORT (AIS)

FOOD SCIENCE

Food production and food export are two important industries in Australia. Science plays a large role in the food industry. Food science involves the application of scientific methods to the development, processing, packaging and distribution of food products from farms to supermarkets.

FOOD TECHNOLOGIST

JOB DESCRIPTION

Food technologists develop new food products and food processing techniques. They improve existing food products and processes. They also set standards for food production and packaging. Food technologists devise techniques to ensure hygienic conditions for the processing, storage and packaging of foods. Food technologists can specialise in areas such as the dairy industry or the seafood industry.

RANGE OF WORK:

- test raw foods and processed foods for nutritional value
- check foods for colour, taste and flavour
- work in laboratories, usually for food processing companies

EDUCATION AND TRAINING

Food technologists need a degree in science or applied science with a major in food science and technology or nutrition. Many food technologists have postgraduate qualifications.

FOOD STANDARDS OFFICER

JOB DESCRIPTION

There are strict hygiene and quality standards in the Australian food industry. There are also extra requirements for Australian foods that are to be exported overseas. Most food standards officers specialise in a particular food product or industry, such as the meat industry or the sugarcane industry. Some work in quarantine, inspecting food products being brought into Australia from overseas.

RANGE OF WORK:

- inspect animals, plants and agricultural produce at farms, abattoirs, processing factories, wholesale markets and shipping docks
- make sure foods meet Government standards

EDUCATION AND TRAINING

Certificate and diploma courses are offered in most states in the various fields such as meat and seafood processing.

FOOD PROCESS WORKER

JOB DESCRIPTION

Food production processes involve machinery. Food process workers operate the machinery and prepare food using a range of equipment and methods.

RANGE OF WORK:

- take samples of food products
- operate and clean conveyor equipment
- prepare and sort foods, such as fruit and vegetables, for processing and feed them into machines
- operate machinery that will blend or freeze foods

EDUCATION AND TRAINING

You can work as a food process worker without formal qualifications as most training occurs on-the-job. However, there are traineeship programs in food processing in most states.

MY STORY

I work with universities, industry and Government to produce long-term benefits for the Australian food industry. I am currently working on increasing Australia's food exports through research into how to add more nutrients into foods.

Sometimes I work in the laboratory, analysing and testing food products. A lot of my work is done on a computer where I analyse the data from my experiments. I am also responsible for presenting that data to industry groups. Another important part of my job is applying for grants for funding for future projects.

A few words of advice:
Food science is an exciting area to work in, but research can be unpredictable, so be prepared for things to go wrong sometimes.

RANJAN SHARMA
SENIOR FOOD SCIENTIST

'research can be unpredictable'

COMPUTER SCIENCE

Computer scientists design computers and the software systems that make them work. They develop information technologies and create ways to adapt computers for new uses. As technology becomes more advanced, demand for computer science jobs is increasing.

• COMPUTER PROGRAMMER

JOB DESCRIPTION

Computer programmers write, test and maintain computer programs to make sure the computer and its programs do the jobs they are required to do.

RANGE OF WORK:

- write program specifications
- research computer users' requirements
- analyse and help solve problems outlined by computer designers
- write and modify programs in a computer language
- test programs and make any changes that might make them run better

EDUCATION AND TRAINING

Computer programmers usually have a diploma or degree in information technology with a major in computer programming. However, this is not always necessary as the emphasis for programming roles is on specific skills which can either be gained through formal education or work experience. Computer programmers need to regularly update their knowledge of the latest technologies.

• COMPUTER SCIENTIST/ ENGINEER

JOB DESCRIPTION

Computer scientists, also known as computer engineers, are involved in the installation, repair and servicing of computers and computer equipment. They can specialise as hardware or software engineers. Computer scientists might work with systems analysts to design the computer hardware or find solutions for problems with computer systems.

EDUCATION AND TRAINING

Computer scientists/engineers require an engineering degree with a major in computer engineering, or a computer science degree.

SYSTEMS ANALYST

JOB DESCRIPTION

Systems analysts research, review, develop and test IT systems. They work closely with computer engineers to research how computer systems are used and look at ways to improve systems and their efficiency for users. Systems analysts also review and develop computer systems, languages and data communication processes.

RANGE OF SPECIALITIES:

- ***applications systems*** – working with businesses to develop specific computer systems and programs
- ***computer testing*** – testing newly built systems
- ***data modelling*** – using data models to show clients various options for computer systems and helping them choose the one most suitable for them
- ***network analysis*** – analysing data flows and technical requirements to design network systems
- ***operation systems analysis*** – analysing the components of systems to improve their performance

EDUCATION AND TRAINING

To become a systems analyst you need to study information technology or computer science at university.

COMPUTER SUPPORT TECHNICIAN

JOB DESCRIPTION

Many people in a variety of fields work using computers and sometimes need people to help them. Computer support technicians provide technical advice and support to help people effectively use computer software and hardware.

RANGE OF WORK:

- identify the computers and software needed in a particular organisation
- provide telephone, in-person and online support to users
- install and download appropriate software
- train staff on how to use the computer and its software

EDUCATION AND TRAINING

Traineeships and apprenticeships are available in this area, although the best way to gain employment is by completing a diploma in computer systems engineering.

'Keep up your maths.'

MY STORY

I am a professor of computer science at the University of Western Australia and my job involves teaching undergraduate classes, supervising postgraduate students and doing my own research. My research involves using mathematical modelling on computers to explore how bushfires and epidemics spread. The models are simulations of the real world and they allow people to predict the movements of bushfires and epidemics. My job also involves a lot of administration work to raise the money needed for research in the department. This can mean that I don't have enough time to do my research. The best thing about working as an academic in this field is the freedom to do my own research on things that are of interest to me.

A few words of advice:
Keep up your maths. Mathematics can play an important part in computer science and give you more job options.

GEORGE MILNE
COMPUTER SCIENTIST

WEATHER SCIENCE

Many people need accurate information about the weather – farmers, hot-air balloonists, pilots, surfers and firefighters, as well as people wondering what to wear in the morning. Weather patterns are studied so that predictions can be made. Physics and mathematics play a large role in many jobs in weather science.

• METEOROLOGICAL TECHNICAL OFFICER

JOB DESCRIPTION

Meteorological technical officers use instruments and gauges attached to weather balloons, and at ground level, to make observations and measurements of climatic and atmospheric conditions. This can include air temperature, wind speed and direction, humidity, rainfall and evaporation. Meteorological technical officers often work with meteorologists in tropical and remote locations. Depending on the duties, the work may be done indoors or outside, in large offices or in small remote field stations.

RANGE OF WORK:

- monitor the surface and upper air meteorological conditions
- develop new systems for weather observations
- distribute statistics, maps, forecasts and other meteorological information to clients and the media

EDUCATION AND TRAINING

To become a meteorological technical officer, you need to study maths, a physical science, computing, or engineering (electronics).

• METEOROLOGIST

JOB DESCRIPTION

Meteorologists use and develop scientific techniques, including highly complex computer models, to forecast and interpret weather conditions. They also study the atmosphere to learn more about how the weather works. Meteorologists present the forecasts for the public and the media. They prepare special forecasts for aviation, agriculture, fishing and shipping, and they issue warnings for cyclones, storms, floods, frosts, fire dangers and gales.

EDUCATION AND TRAINING

To become a meteorologist, you need a degree in environmental sciences, mathematics, geography, physical sciences, physics, meteorology, or a related field. Graduate meteorologists at the Bureau of Meteorology complete a training program before being posted to a regional or field office.

AEROSPACE ENGINEER

JOB DESCRIPTION

Aerospace engineers perform and supervise design, development, manufacture and maintenance work on all types of flight vehicles. This can include aeroplanes and helicopters, missiles, launch vehicles, spacecraft and satellites, as well as control and guidance systems. In Australia, the majority of aerospace engineering work involves aircraft modification and assessment of damage.

EDUCATION AND TRAINING

To become an aerospace engineer, you must have studied engineering at university with a major in aeronautical or aerospace engineering.

MY STORY

I work at the Bureau of Meteorology in Melbourne. I completed a science degree in New South Wales with honours in physics and maths. I've always loved science, especially physics. After uni I applied to the training program with the Bureau and studied for nine months as a trainee meteorologist. I have worked in Canberra, Sydney, Darwin (after Cyclone Tracy) and Melbourne.

My main role as senior forecaster is to coordinate the putting together of the forecasts from the weather data. We forecast weather for the general public, the media, the CFA (Country Fire Authority), airports and various industries. I also draw weather charts. When I first started working as a meteorologist I was terrible at it. There is a definite art to drawing charts, which you learn and perfect with time. I like the shift work involved in my job because it means that I don't have a strict nine to five routine. I also enjoy working with a talented team of meteorologists. And I get great pleasure out of providing a service to the community that helps people make decisions. One of the highlights of my career was forecasting the weather in Sydney during the Sydney Olympic Games in 2000. It was a fantastic experience to work on such an important event.

A few words of advice:
You've got to be enthusiastic about science, particularly maths and physics. Work experience can also provide great learning opportunities.

TERRY RYAN
SENIOR FORECASTER

'You've got to be enthusiastic about science'

ANIMALS AND SCIENCE

There is a variety of jobs that combine science and working with animals. Some jobs involve caring for sick or injured animals, others focus on studying animals, and some involve using and caring for animals in scientific research.

VETERINARIAN

JOB DESCRIPTION

Veterinarians (vets) diagnose and treat sickness, disease and injury in all types of animals, from cats to cows. They advise farmers on ways to improve the health and productivity of animals, and they give pet owners advice on keeping their pets healthy. Vets can work either indoors or outdoors depending on the location of the animals they are treating. Vets usually work long and irregular hours, especially those in private practice who can be called upon to treat sick animals at any hour of the day or night.

RANGE OF WORK:

- examine sick and injured animals
- perform tests and examine tissue samples from sick animals to identify the causes of diseases
- treat animals using drugs, surgical procedures and nursing care

EDUCATION AND TRAINING

To be a vet you must have completed a veterinary science degree. Specialised roles such as those working with wildlife or livestock may need postgraduate qualifications.

VETERINARY NURSE

JOB DESCRIPTION

Veterinary nurses assist veterinarians in the treatment and care of animals needing medical and/or surgical attention.

RANGE OF WORK:

- monitor sick animals
- clean animals before surgery
- sterilise equipment
- reception duties including answering the telephone, making appointments and taking payments

EDUCATION AND TRAINING

A certificate in veterinary nursing is usually the minimum requirement for employment as a veterinary nurse.

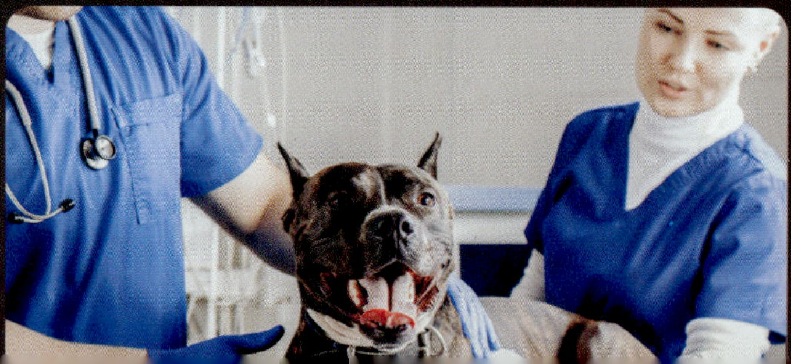

WILDLIFE OFFICER

JOB DESCRIPTION

Wildlife officers are responsible for the animals in national parks, scenic areas, nature reserves and other recreational areas. Wildlife officers are often involved in the breeding programs of endangered animals. They also assist in wildlife management projects, including surveys and monitoring of wildlife.

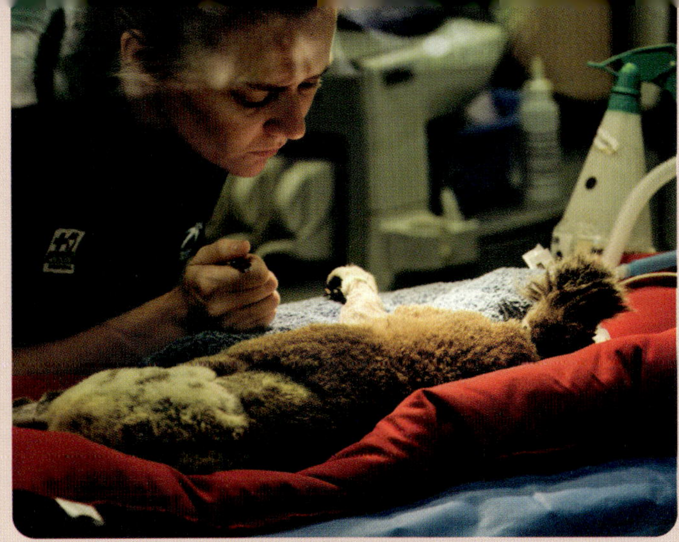

EDUCATION AND TRAINING

You can work as a wildlife officer without formal qualifications. However, entry to this job might be improved if you have qualifications and/or work experience. A TAFE certificate in captive animals, or conservation and land management will improve your job prospects.

'Be prepared to get dirty'

MY STORY

Vets do an amazing range of things, including research, determining animal welfare policies, and working in quarantine to protect the health of Australian people and livestock. Most people start out studying veterinary science because they see themselves doing the classic vet work – dealing with people's dogs, cats, horses and cattle, etc. People have a huge variety of other pets, such as ferrets, snakes, rats, rabbits, lizards and birds, and they will bring them to you!

Working as a vet can be a physically demanding and dangerous job. For instance, when you put your arm in the rectum of a horse, you run the risk that it might move and break your arm, or kick back and hurt you. Any dog could bite you and many cats will scratch you.

Vets need to have a lot of scientific knowledge, but they don't need to be a science genius to be a good vet. It is not all about cuddling cute little puppies and playing with kittens, although that is an occasional bonus.

A few words of advice:
Be prepared to get dirty, to work long hours, to get injured occasionally, to put animals to sleep and to cry about it. But also be prepared to feel the thrill of doing something that is important and valuable to our society and improves the welfare of animals.

RIATI HENDRATA
VETERINARIAN

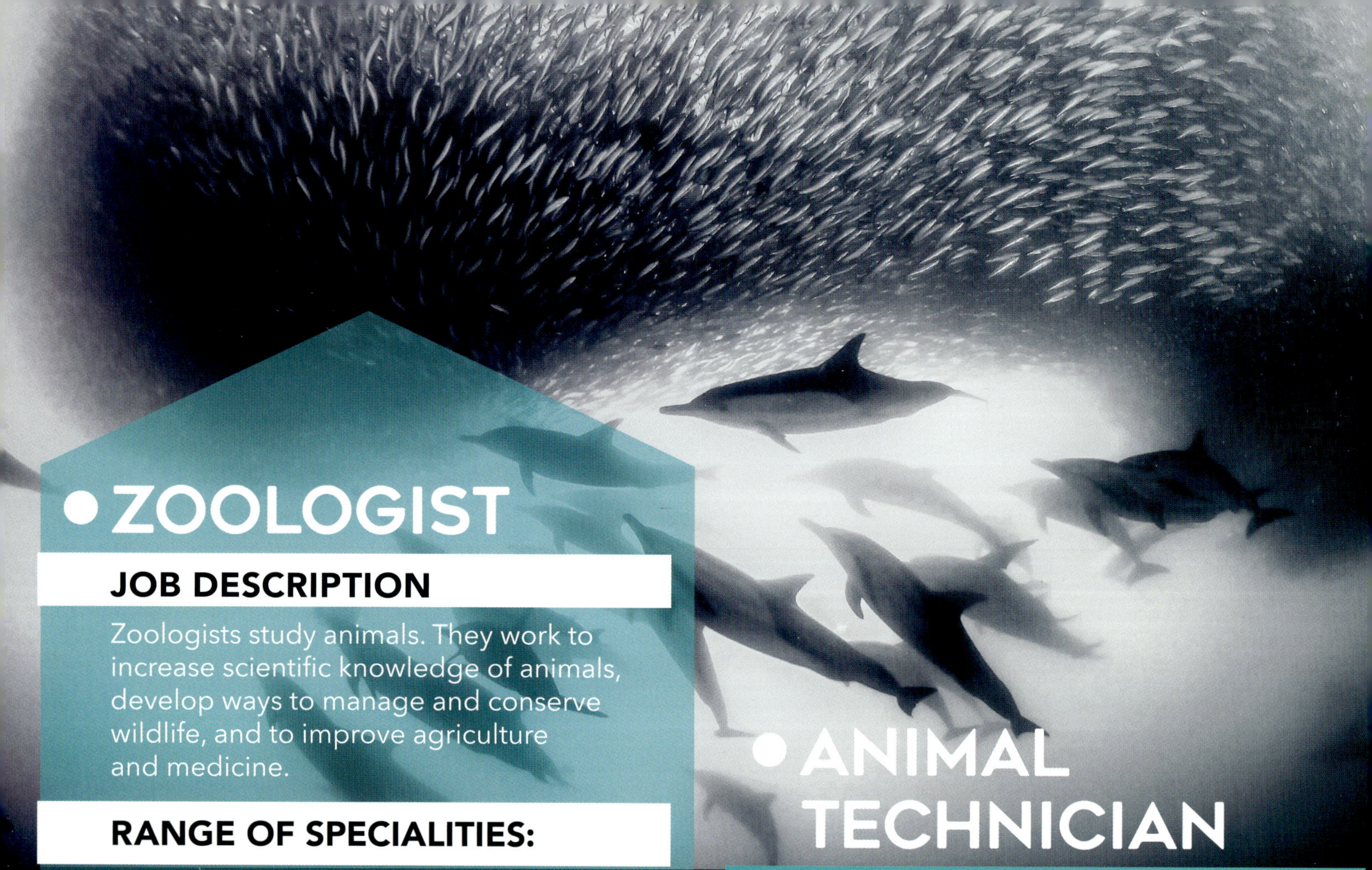

ZOOLOGIST

JOB DESCRIPTION

Zoologists study animals. They work to increase scientific knowledge of animals, develop ways to manage and conserve wildlife, and to improve agriculture and medicine.

RANGE OF SPECIALITIES:

- ***entomology*** - insects
- ***parasitology*** - internal and external parasites
- ***ecology*** - environment of animals
- ***ethology*** - animal behaviour
- ***ichthyology*** - fish
- ***mammalogy*** - mammals
- ***ornithology*** - birds
- ***herpetology*** - reptiles and amphibians
- ***physiology*** - how animals' bodies function

RANGE OF WORK:

- investigate the relationships between animals and their environment by studying animals in their natural surroundings or in captivity
- perform experiments to identify species and gather information on animals' growth, nutritional needs, reproduction, prey and predators
- study the development and anatomy of animals to develop methods of population control in certain species

EDUCATION AND TRAINING

A degree in science or applied science with a major in zoology is the minimum requirement for becoming a zoologist. However, postgraduate study is generally needed to work in this field as you are expected to specialise in one of the above areas.

ANIMAL TECHNICIAN

JOB DESCRIPTION

Animal technicians help scientists to care for and observe the animals used for research purposes. All animal technicians must obey strict rules and guidelines for the treatment of animals for research, devised by the ethics committee at their place of employment.

RANGE OF WORK:

- check and record the health status and behaviour of animals in their care
- prepare food and water for the animals
- carry out experiments using the animals
- take samples from the animals
- clean and disinfect cages and help with injections and surgery on the animals

EDUCATION AND TRAINING

Animal technicians require a TAFE certificate or diploma related to the handling of captive animals or animal technology.

ANIMAL ATTENDANT

JOB DESCRIPTION

Animal attendants feed, water and care for animals used for scientific research.

RANGE OF WORK:

- clean and prepare comfortable sleeping quarters for animals
- clear away animal waste
- clean, disinfect and look after animal enclosures and cages
- bathe and groom animals, and treat them with insecticides to control insect pests
- treat minor injuries and report serious health problems to veterinarians
- assist with the humane killing of animals and handling of animals that have died
- maintain animal records

EDUCATION AND TRAINING

You can work as an animal attendant on completion of Year 10, with some informal training provided on-the-job. However, a TAFE certificate related to laboratory animal technology will improve employment chances.

'Work experience is always good'

MY STORY

Animal welfare is the main focus of my job. I need to make sure all our mice remain healthy and continue breeding, and that any sick animals are treated promptly. I have been an animal technician for more than 10 years and my primary role now is training. I train the technicians in basic animal care, such as how to clean animal boxes, feeding, watering, health checking and breeding. When they are skilled in these areas, I teach them the more difficult tasks such as organ removal, blood collection and injections. I also sit on the animal ethics committee that considers applications by scientists to use animals in their research.

A few words of advice:
Work experience is always good because it shows that you are dedicated and want to work with animals.

JULIE MERRYFULL
SENIOR ANIMAL TECHNICIAN

SOCIAL SCIENCES

The social sciences involve the study of human behaviour, societies and social patterns. The social sciences aim to describe how people interact with each other and with the world around them.

FORENSIC SCIENTIST

JOB DESCRIPTION

A forensic scientist is someone who analyses evidence in order to investigate crime. Forensic scientists analyse physical evidence left at crime scenes. This can include biological evidence, such as blood, hair and DNA, as well as illicit drugs and other substances. They also write reports and give evidence in court. Forensic scientists usually specialise in one area, such as crime scene examination, firearms examination or toxicology.

EDUCATION AND TRAINING

Forensic scientist jobs are rare and this is a hard area to find employment in. Forensic scientists need an degree in science with a major related to forensics. Most forensic scientists have postgraduate qualifications.

POLITICAL SCIENTIST

JOB DESCRIPTION

Political scientists study the theory, origin, development and functioning of political parties, unions and other groups such as environmental or human rights groups. They also examine individual, group and mass behaviours and their relationship to society and the economy. Political scientists work in universities and Government departments, as well as for political parties.

RANGE OF WORK:

- research areas such as political philosophy
- assemble research data by consulting and studying the works of others and observing political institutions
- analyse data and draw conclusions
- present findings and conclusions for publication or use by Government, political parties, international institutions and non-Government organisations
- write articles for daily papers and journals

EDUCATION AND TRAINING

To become a political scientist you need to complete an arts degree with a major in politics or political science. Jobs in this field are very competitive and postgraduate study will improve employment opportunities.

SOCIOLOGIST

JOB DESCRIPTION

A sociologist studies society, social patterns and the way social groups interact. They do this by observing people, collecting and analysing data, interpreting facts and figures and interviewing people. Sociologists must have good research skills, excellent oral and written communication skills and an interest in social issues. Sociologists work in universities and Government departments.

EDUCATION AND TRAINING

To become a sociologist, you need to study arts or social sciences at university with a major in sociology. Most sociologists complete postgraduate qualifications in order to be able to conduct independent research, rather that just assisting a more senior academic.

MY STORY

Politics is such a fascinating field that I knew I had to be a political scientist because I certainly didn't want to be a politician. I studied politics at high school and university, and always wrote articles for the local newspaper. I have worked for the Government and various political parties and universities. I now work in Geneva for the United Nations, and research the role Governments play in human rights issues.

A few words of advice:
It really is interesting work though you have to love research and communicating. You also have to keep up with everything that is happening in politics and current affairs, both in Australia and overseas.

JULIE SHRADER
POLITICAL SCIENTIST

'It really is interesting work'

SCIENCE IN THE MEDIA

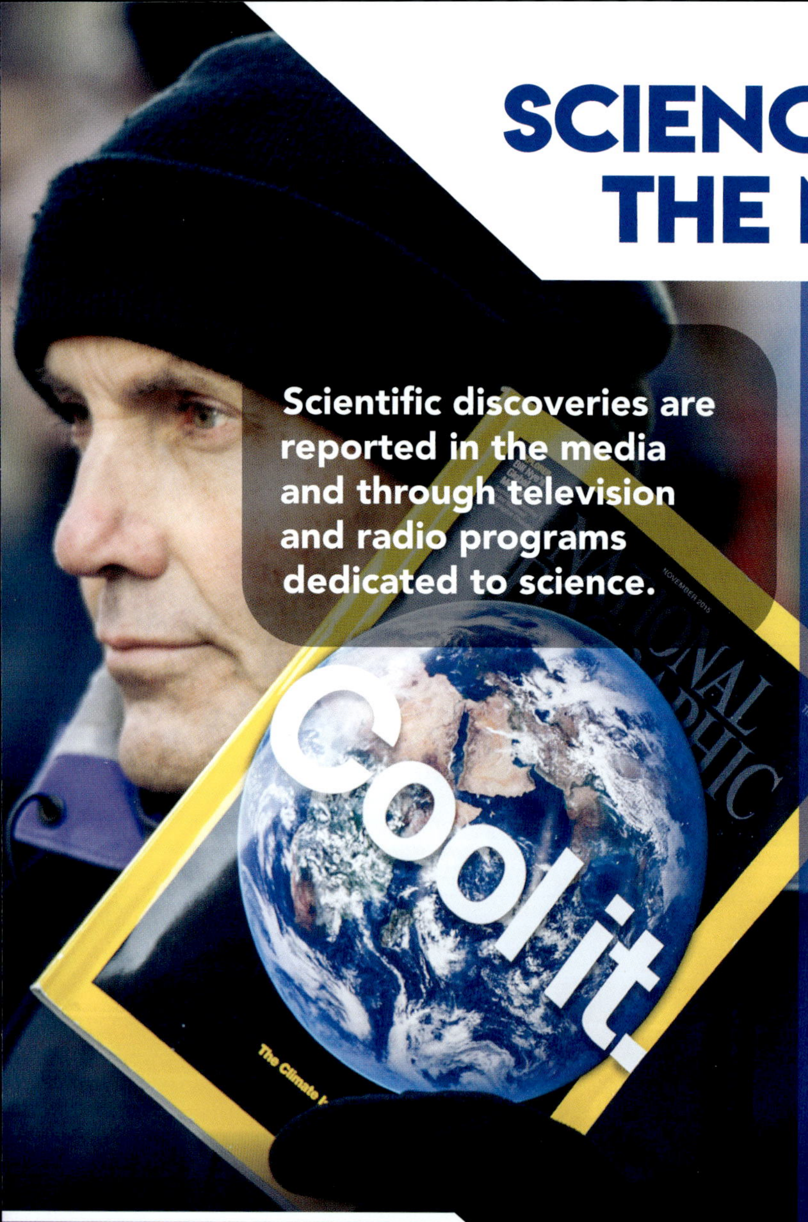

Scientific discoveries are reported in the media and through television and radio programs dedicated to science.

SCIENCE REPORTER

JOB DESCRIPTION

Science reporters write and edit news reports, commentaries and features for newspapers, magazines, radio, or television. They present complex scientific material in a simple way so that people who are not scientists can understand it. Science reporters interview scientists, attend scientific events and research background information. They choose which scientific news to report, depending on which stories they feel will be most appealling to non-scientists.

EDUCATION AND TRAINING

Science reporters do not require a science degree, but it can be an advantage. Most science reporters have studied journalism and started work as a cadet at a newspaper, or at a radio or television station. After the initial cadet training, showing an interest in science can help you to become a science reporter.

'Take a general interest in science'

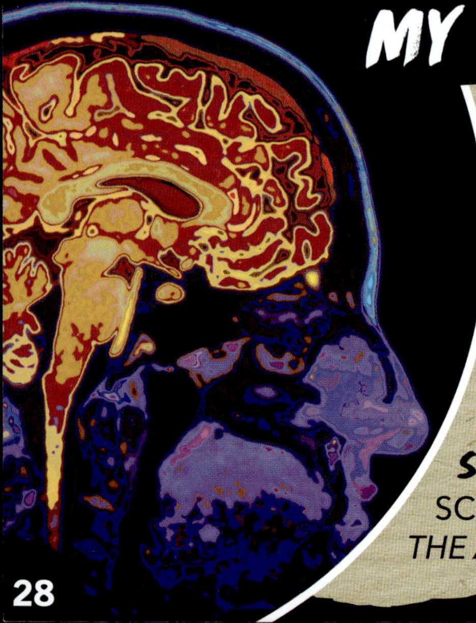

MY STORY

I have been interested in science since primary school - things like astronomy, space flight, dinosaurs, nuclear fusion and time travel. I started work as a casual reporter at a local newspaper, then I got a cadetship at The Age in Melbourne. For the first few years I covered mostly general news, before I managed to join The Age's health and science team.

I am not required to do scientific research, or write papers for journals. My job is that of a middleman - selecting stories that may be of interest to people and then writing them in a way that people can understand. There are two important things to have as a science reporter. One is a flair for communication, such as writing, or talking. The other is an interest in the type of science stories people like.

A few words of advice:
Take a general interest in science as a broad field and remember that science reporting is all about choosing science stories that people will be interested in.

STEVE CAUCHI
SCIENCE REPORTER
THE AGE

SCIENCE ADMINISTRATION

• GRANTS OFFICER

JOB DESCRIPTION

A grant is a sum of money that the Government or a private organisation pays for work it thinks will benefit the community. Grants officers read, review and edit grant applications made by scientists before they are sent to the organisation offering the grant. They help scientists to express themselves clearly and ensure that non-specialists can understand the science behind the application.

EDUCATION AND TRAINING

There is no specific course in this field, but a science degree and good communication skills can help gain employment.

• PERSONAL ASSISTANT

JOB DESCRIPTION

Personal assistants help scientists plan their appointments, organise travel arrangements, type letters and schedule meetings. They might also type up reports, photocopy and perform any other tasks that will help the scientist.

EDUCATION AND TRAINING

Not all personal assistants have formal qualifications, but job opportunities are increased with a certificate in business or office administration. Many scientists like to have personal assistants with an interest in science.

MY STORY

Grant applications are so important because many scientists rely on them for funding. Without a grant, a lot of scientific work would not go ahead. My main role is to read, review and edit all grant applications made by scientists. I have a PhD in endocrinology and my science background helps me understand what scientists are trying to say in their applications. It is my job to make sure they convey what their research involves and the importance of their research. I need to know the processes and policies of all the grants and the date the applications are due. The grant application process can be very stressful for scientists and they are under a lot of pressure.

I like my job because I get to know a lot of the scientists and I become familiar with the work they are doing. I love it when people are successful with their grant applications. I don't like having to tell people their grant application has been unsuccessful.

A few words of advice:
I have found my science background has helped me in my position as there is a lot of science knowledge required in grant applications.

JULIE MERCER
GRANTS OFFICER

'there is a lot of science in grant applications'

GET FUTURE READY

If you think you might be interested in a career in science, there are a few things that you can do right now that might be useful later. Why not research your education pathways to see what options are available to you? Maybe you could plan the qualification route that you might like to follow, or investigate the practical steps you could take to gain experience in the types of work that interest you.

THE FUTURE

PRACTICAL EXPERIENCE

- find work experience in a relevant scientific area
- talk to people who work in similar jobs
- read as much as you can about the job
- check what qualifications are needed
- research the job on the Internet
- Find out if your school has a Science Club you could join. If not, why not talk to your science teacher about starting one.

DO YOU NEED QUALIFICATIONS?

There are many different levels of qualifications and training opportunities for jobs in science. Some jobs in science can be entered into straight from secondary school, but most require TAFE certificates, diplomas and often a university degree. Senior scientists in most fields have postgraduate qualifications. The science field is competitive, so the more qualifications you have, the more likely you are to get a job in your chosen field. At school, you can keep your options open by doing a variety of science subjects.

GLOSSARY

biomechanics study of how muscles, bones and tendons work together as athletes move

data flows way information is used and passed from one computer system to another

data modelling using computer programs to demonstrate something, such as bushfire spread

DNA molecules inside cells that determine their genetic make-up

endocrinology study of hormones and how they relate to functions in the body

epidemic rapid spread of a disease from person to person, or animal to animal

ethics accepted principles for behaviour

force plates plates that measure the force of an athlete's feet hitting the ground as they run

grants funds for research from the Government or other industry body

hardware physical components of a computer, such as the monitor and microchips

hydrology science dealing with water on the land or under the Earth's surface

IT systems computer software, hardware and networking systems required by an organisation

neuropsychology branch of psychology dealing with the brain and nervous system

ore metal-bearing mineral or rock

physiology study of the way living things function

quarantine checking of animals and plants for disease as they come into the country, and keeping them isolated if necessary to prevent the spread of diseases

radiotherapy treatment for cancer that involves using radiation to kill cancerous cells

rock cores samples of rocks taken by drilling out a long cylinder from deep in the rock

scientific methods taking an idea and investigating it by designing and conducting an experiment, making observations, recording and testing results, interpreting the results and drawing conclusions

seismic testing setting off small explosions and measuring the resulting vibrations

shift work work that is done late at night or on weekends and public holidays

software programs needed to run a computer application

TAFE Technical And Further Education

telemetry systems high-speed radio systems which allow data to be transmitted

toxicology scientific study of poisons

vaccine modified version of a disease that makes the body immune to that disease

INDEX